– A 28-DAY DEVOTIONAL FOR MOMS –

Abundant Fruit

CULTIVATING FRUIT OF THE SPIRIT THROUGH SPIRITUAL GROWTH

CASEY WAYNE

Abundant Fruit: Cultivating Fruit of the Spirit Through Spiritual Growth
By Casey Wayne

Copyright © 2022 by Casey Wayne

Requests for information can be sent to: casey@peaceoffaith.org.

All scripture quotations are taken from Holy Bible, New Living Translation, copyright © 1996, 2004, 2007 by Tyndale House Foundation. Used by permission of Tyndale House Publishers, Inc., Carol Stream, Illinois 60188. All rights reserved.

ISBN 979-8-9860183-0-0 (print)
ISBN 979-8-9860183-1-7 (ebook)

Copy Editing by Abbey Espinoza
Book cover and interior design by Vanessa Mendozzi

CONTENTS

Introduction

Dear friend,
When I was at my lowest and grasping for next steps, God revealed the fruit of the Spirit to me. Over the years, Galatians 5:22-25 has become a guiding source for what my life should look like as I strive to be more like Jesus to those around me.

I pray that this devotional truly blesses you and helps you grow in your faith. Even as a Christ follower, life can be tough. Days can still be filled with chaos, and our human instincts can bring us down. However, I am so thankful for the mighty God we worship—His kindness, grace, and hope for our lives. My hope is that you will experience a closer walk with God and learn how to allow the Holy Spirit to work in and through you in everyday life.

I invite you to open your eyes and ears to what God reveals to you as you read each devotion. Pray that he will soften your soul to prepare it for molding and reveal areas that you need to lift to your heavenly Father. God is waiting for you to pursue a deeper relationship with him so that he can give you peace and righteousness all the days of your life.

Blessing to you,

Casey

Accept the Spirit and Share the Fruit

"But the Holy Spirit produces this kind of fruit in our lives: love, joy, peace, patience, kindness, goodness, faithfulness, gentleness, self-control. There is no law against these things! Those who belong to Christ Jesus have nailed the passions and desires of their sinful nature to his cross and crucified them there. Since we are living by the Spirit, let us follow the Spirit's leading in every part of our lives." (Galatians 5:22-25)

As a young adult navigating how best to create the life I had envisioned, I found myself hitting my first big crisis of faith. I was holding so tightly to my plan for my life that I was unwilling and unable to see what God had in mind. Desperate for what to do next, I dropped to my knees, and with tears streaming down my face, I asked God what he wanted from me. In that moment, He sent the fruit of the Spirit to my mind. I was begging him for a clear plan for my life, and this is what he gave me—A simple call to be faithful and produce fruit for his glory.

Paul wrote to the Galatians who were arguing over how they should live. Like me, they were hungry for a clear vision showing them how to move forward. What should a life for Christ look like? Paul encourages us to allow the Holy Spirit to guide us. As Christ followers, we are sanctified and called to God's purposes through the Holy Spirit. We cannot be passive bystanders in this process. Instead spiritual growth is meant to be an active pursuit. Our sinful nature constantly pulls us into temptation. Satan will look for ways to keep you from pursuing your relationship with your heavenly Father.

But, fortunately, the Holy Spirit gives us the wisdom and guidance to overcome this. Everyone's faith journey will be different. God will call each of us to use our varied gifts for his glory. What we all have in common, however, is that through this process we should be producing fruit! As we become more mature in our faith, we will share that fruit with others, ultimately drawing ourselves and others closer to Jesus.

CHALLENGE:

Are you allowing God to work in you and through you? Ask God to reveal anything in you that is not bringing Him glory.

Love

2

Love All

"So now I am giving you a new commandment: Love each other. Just as I have loved you. Your love for one another will prove to the world that you are my disciples."
(John 13:34-35)

Living with young children can get hectic in a hurry. I sometimes forget to do things or grab things for my daughter when she asks. Sometimes I am even harsh or rude in tone. When I recognize this in myself, I apologize. In response to my apology, she tends to say, "It's okay, Mom. I still love you."

In that moment, this sweet, young girl is sharing grace. She reminds me that I am still loved, even when I make a mistake. She forgives completely with her child's heart, and in doing so she epitomizes the way that God wants us to love others.

God created us with a need to be loved, to receive love. Unfortunately, sometimes we find ourselves unable to share that love with others. Satan convinces us that people should earn our love. He even distorts our minds into thinking that some people don't deserve love at all. They aren't "worthy." However, Jesus commanded his disciples to "love all" before his crucifixion. Our love for others is meant to set us apart as Christ-followers. Even when it feels undeserved or painful, Christ asks us to share his love with everyone, not just those we choose, so they may know him better.

There are some very unloving people in the world. We have all come across our fair share of them. Even when we try to reach out and be kind, they may continue in their ways, making our efforts feel futile. The call to love **all** becomes an uphill struggle. However, through prayer and experience, I have come to realize that people who hurt are generally the ones who hurt others in return. They lash out in anger or frustration, often because they feel deep hurt inside themselves. Their pain has pulled them into a place of darkness. In these circumstances, Christ calls us to be a light in the darkness, even if we never see the fruits of our labor. The simple reality is that it takes strength and courage to love.

1 Peter 3:8-9 says *"Finally all of you should be of one mind. Sympathize with each other as brothers and sisters. Be tender-hearted, and keep a humble attitude. Don't repay evil for evil. Don't retaliate with insults when people insult you. Instead, pay them back with a blessing. That is what God has called you to do, and he will bless you for it."* We are all loved by God as his creation, made in his image. When we choose not to love all those around us, we are demonstrating pride. And that pride will separate us from God. Satan pushes us toward hatred, but God pulls us toward love. Luckily, to find the strength and courage to love **all** we don't have to depend on our own flesh. Instead, we can rely on the outpouring of love we receive from our heavenly Father. If we ask, God

will give us the vision to see others as he sees them. In his eyes, there are no degrees of love. No hierarchy of worth. Jesus sacrificed his life for every single person with equal care for their salvation and heart.

CHALLENGE:

Is there someone you have been struggling to love? Lift that person up to God and ask for the strength and wisdom to see how best to love him or her.

3

Love in Action

"The end of the world is coming soon. Therefore, be earnest and disciplined in your prayers. Most important of all, continue to show deep love for each other, for love covers a multitude of sins. Cheerfully share your home with those who need a meal or a place to stay. God has given each of you a gift from his great variety of gifts. Use them well to serve others."
(1 Peter 4:7-10)

Soon after my husband and I were married, I began to realize my weaknesses when it comes to showing love. Through the years since, I have gradually discovered the things that I tend to say or do that make my husband feel unloved. I'm still working on overcoming these tendencies, and I anticipate that I will need to grapple with these for the rest of our marriage. But navigating those issues has forced me to become more self-aware; I now see more clearly how I express love in my relationships.

I am so thankful that God offers each of us the gifts of unconditional love and grace. These gifts, along with the strength and guidance of the Holy Spirit, allow us to pour into others with the abundance God has given us. This is what paves the way for us to share his love with everyone around us.

Love others and love them well is a clear command from our God. We are called to be the *"hands and feet"* of the Father (Romans 10:14-17). God expects us to love people with our actions as well as with our words. In his kindness, he has blessed each of us with certain skills and resources needed to spread the gospel. You may not be a good teacher, but perhaps you have been given the gift of organization. You can use that skill to show God's love to others. Cooking for the sick, providing words of comfort, teaching, leading, writing, painting, dancing, or computer skills—we all have talents we can share, and we can harness those talents to love and support others for God's glory.

Remember that as Christ-followers, the most important way we can demonstrate God's love to his people is by serving them as he serves us. There are countless examples in the Bible where Jesus modeled how we should be serving others in love. It could be making them a meal after they lost a loved one, offering a listening ear so they can feel seen and heard, texting someone to let them know you were thinking of them, or maybe providing hope and encouragement through your social media. To fully love those around us requires intentional action. It means we have to lean into what our heavenly Father offers us and then share that love with others.

CHALLENGE:

What skill can you use to love others well? Is there someone specific God is putting on your heart and mind who needs some love or support?

4

God's Love

"Don't be afraid, for I am with you. Don't be discouraged for I am your God. I will strengthen you and help you. I will hold you up with my victorious hand."
(Isaiah 41:10)

During a time of unemployment in the early stages of my career, I was lost and adrift. I felt that everything was falling apart around me. However, it was also a time when I drew closest to God. In my broken state, I cried out to our heavenly Father. Despite my disobedience in trying to take control of my future, instead of putting it in his hands, he welcomed me with open arms. In the light of his conviction on my life, I experienced overwhelming love, a love that gave me peace and comfort. It assured me that he would be faithful to me if I would simply step into what he had planned for me.

The love from God is where it all begins, and that love gives us everything we need. His grace and forgiveness, the sacrifice of his Son for our salvation, and the strength he imparts for our sanctification all flow from the knowledge that he first loved us. First John 4:9-10 says, "*God showed how much he loved us by sending his one and only Son into the World so that we might have eternal life through him. This is real love—not that we loved God, but that he loved us and sent his Son as a sacrifice to take away our sins.*" Nothing we do can diminish the love God has for us. Our identity as a child of God gives us the strength and encouragement to live out our faith for his glory.

God sees you and your heart. Your achievements and your struggles. Your faith and your doubt. Dive into his Word and allow his love to fill the depths of your soul like nothing else will. The grace and hope found through Jesus restores and strengthens. If you feel as though you are treading water in the chaos of life, know that he offers us peace and rest in him. Even Jesus took time to rest during his journeys here on Earth. God calls us to rest in him, saying "*Be still and know I am God*" (Psalm 46:10).

Whether you are only starting to recognize the depth of God's love for us or are a seasoned warrior for Christ, we all have moments in our faith walk where we must sit at the feet of Jesus and allow him to restore our hearts and reveal our next steps. Remind yourself today of God's faithfulness, love, and provision for you thus far. Sink into the depths of his love, hope, and peace, taking a deep breath and soaking it all in. Pray for your next steps and how he will call you to share his amazing, overwhelming love with others.

CHALLENGE:

Spend time today reminding yourself of God's love and faithfulness. Make a list of all the answered prayers and blessings he has provided you. Pray a prayer of thanksgiving and ask him to reveal to you opportunities to share his love with others.

5

Joy Compared to Happiness

"I pray that God, the source of hope, will fill you completely with joy and peace because you trust in him. Then you will overflow with confident hope through the power of the Holy Spirit." (Romans 15:13)

For a long time, I believed that if I could just reach the goals I had set for my life, then I would be happy. Each day, week and year was centered on controlling my circumstances to create the perfect life filled with happiness. However, the more I chased this idea of happiness through the world's standards, the more conflicted I felt inside. Why weren't these accomplishments making me happy, making me feel calmer? We all want to feel like we can reach a place of inner peace in a world of chaos. But where we tend to trip up is when we strive for man-made happiness instead of seeking true joy in Christ. I discovered that searching for fulfillment from the world, instead of placing my hope in my Creator, could never fill the void in my soul.

Happiness is a fleeting emotion based on our circumstances. I know my happiness can quickly dissipate when

I discover a mess my kids made or when I can't get my to-do list done. However, we must remember that there is a vast difference in temporary happiness and true, lasting biblical JOY! The joy we receive through God's words and promises creates an inner peace, even when we are unhappy with our circumstances. It is the assurance that God is in control and the belief that he will work everything for our good. When you rest in the knowledge and hope of God's faithfulness, the Spirit will fill your heart with peace, even in the storms of life.

If you are struggling to find the peace and joy God offers us, ask him to reveal it to you. Read his Word, reminding yourself of times he has been faithful. Step out in faith where he leads, trusting that his plan is always greater than what we could come up with. He offers us overflowing confidence in who he is and a peace that *surpasses all understanding*" (Philippians 4:7). God's joy is like nothing this world can give. It will fill you with an unending source of hope, no matter what life brings you.

CHALLENGE:

How has God shown you his faithfulness? Ask him to fill you with the joy that comes from his peace in your life.

6

Joy in the Storm

"I know the Lord is always with me. I will not be shaken, for he is right beside me. No wonder my heart is glad, and I rejoice. My body rests in safety."
(Psalm 16:8-9)

When I left my teaching job to become a stay-at-home mom, it was not under ideal circumstances. God had already been planting the seed in both my heart and my husband's for me to consider staying home once our second child was born that upcoming summer. Then circumstances at work changed at the start of the spring semester. I was placed in a position that threatened my physical safety as a pregnant woman within the classroom. After multiple conversations with school administrators, they concluded that they could not offer me any alternative options. We prayerfully, and quickly, had to make the decision that I would resign and start life as a stay-at-home mom sooner than anticipated. It was not easy, but I knew it was ultimately God's plan for me when, through tears, I experienced an overwhelming peace as I submitted my resignation letter. In the years to come, God gave me more peace and passion for life as a stay-at-home Mom, eventually revealing more of his plan to use my skills in other ways for his glory.

We all want a peaceful, happy life. But the reality is that God does not promise us a life without hardships. The devil will fight to steal our joy (John 10:10) and distract us from all the good things that God has for us. Life brings with it sorrow, pain, and confusion that can damage our souls. Even though we may not be happy in our current circumstance or phase of life, God is an unending source of true joy, even when life falls apart.

When you find yourself in the depths of darkness that life inevitably brings, remember that God is our ultimate source of help. Psalm 28:6-7 says, *"Praise the Lord! For he has heard my cry for mercy. The Lord is my strength and shield. I trust him with all my heart. He helps me, and my heart is filled with joy. I burst out in songs of thanksgiving."* Lean into your relationship with your heavenly Father, for he has shown himself to be faithful to provide all that we need—even what we never realized we needed. God is not absent in the storm. He is there with you, if you will only reach out to him. He will turn your sorrow into joy by providing everything you need (Psalm 30:11-12).

CHALLENGE:

Name three moments in your life when you remember God was with you and for you. Pray for the strength to endure the storm and the wisdom to know how to navigate it.

7

Spreading Comfort and Joy

"All praise to God, the Father of our Lord Jesus Christ. God is our merciful Father and the source of all comfort. He comforts us in all our troubles so that we can comfort others. When they are troubled, we will be able to give them the same comfort God has given us." (2 Corinthians 1:3-4)

I love to cook and host people, much like my mother has for years. And when my mother cooks, she always cooks a variety and an abundance of dishes. It has been impressed upon her heart to bring joy to people by serving them in that way. The food may simply be hamburgers or a Crockpot of soup, but her goal is for everyone to feel seen and loved. Nothing fancy required, just providing an atmosphere of hospitality that allows others to feel at home brings her great happiness.

That is how I imagine spreading God's comfort and joy should be—nothing flashy, merely sharing my heart with others. The power lies in its simplicity. Through our faith, we have received a comfort, hope, and strength that cannot be matched by anything this world provides. In Second Thessalonians 2:16, Paul reminds believers that God

graciously *"gave us eternal comfort and wonderful hope."*
Paul is stressing to us here that what God provides is more
than enough; his provision is, in fact, the only thing that
will bring eternal joy.

Serve well those whom God places in your path. Pray for
God to make you aware of those who need to be comforted
and how best to serve them. And when others take notice of
your strength and joy even in the midst of your struggles,
point them in the direction of the source. Peter made it clear
when he said, *"You must worship Christ as Lord of your life.
And if someone asks about your Christian hope, always be
ready to explain it."* (1 Peter 3:15)

CHALLENGE:

Is there someone God has been laying on your heart to comfort or
to share your source of joy? Pray that he will reveal anyone to you
that needs to hear how you have experienced this through Him.

Peace

8

More Peace, Less Fear

"But when I am afraid, I will put my trust in you. I praise God for what he has promised. I trust God, so why should I be afraid? What can mere mortals do to me?"
(Psalm 56:3-4)

After my first pregnancy ended in a miscarriage, I was terrified. I spent many sleepless nights questioning God's plan. Endless uncertainties filled my mind regarding my ability to carry and give birth to a child in the future. I'd often try to convince myself that if I just planned ahead or did other things to try to control the outcome that I would feel better. Of course, none of that ever worked. The fear was still a constant weight over my daily life.

Fear is possibly the most powerful and crippling emotion we experience. Fear, anxiety, and worry can pull us to react in ways we would not have done otherwise—and Satan knows this. Our mind becomes a battlefield that ultimately influences our heart and our actions. The devil strives to lead our thoughts and deeds away from our heavenly Father (2 Corinthians 11:3). But we can also choose to live in confidence that when we seek God's strength and peace, it will always be there for us.

In the book of Romans, Paul instructs us on how to live in the Spirit. Romans 8:6 says, *"So letting your sinful nature control your mind leads to death. But letting the Spirit control your mind leads to life and peace."* By calling on the Holy Spirit, we can live in the peace and strength God offers us. We are called to pray and give our worries to him, staying alert to the devil's attempts to attack (1 Peter 5:7). This concept is often summed up with the phrase "Faith over fear."

God calls us to lean into him in times of temptation and fear. All our hope and trust should be placed in him. Our heavenly Father is faithful to provide us **all** we need and to ultimately give us the strength to flee from the temptations laid out by Satan (James 4:7). Rest in who God is and in the certainty that he has an amazing plan for your life. Freedom from fear, anxiety, and worry can be found in the peace of knowing He will give you what you seek if you will only pursue your relationship with him.

CHALLENGE:

Have you given up your fear, worry, and anxiety to God? Pray that God will reveal to you areas where you are allowing the enemy to pull you away from the relationship with your heavenly Father.

9

God's Peace

"I have told you all this so that you may have peace in me. Here on earth you will have many trials and sorrows. But take heart, because I have overcome the world."
(John 16:33)

As a young adult, I felt confident in the plan I had for my life. Go to college, get a job using my degree, get married, and eventually start a family. I was naive and clung tightly to my vision of who I should be. The harder I fought for the future that I thought God wanted for me, the less peace I felt about that future. Things got confusing, and nothing seemed to be working out the way I envisioned. And in full honesty, I was getting mad at God because of it. I was certain he would want to bless me with the future I wanted.

This all eventually led to a moment with God where I fell to my knees, ready to give up. Instead of giving him my future from the beginning, I had ignored him and tried to make him fit into my plan. In his kindness, God finally brought me to a moment of clarity. To get the peace I was searching for, I had to be "all in" with him and his plans, not mine. Since taking the giant leap of faith to give it all to him, I have felt a peace like nothing I ever experienced before. Even through the chaos of life and transitioning from early marriage to becoming a family of four (with all *that* brings), I have been able to rest in the peace of God.

God is ready to give us his amazing peace that *"surpasses all understanding"* (Philippians 4:7). With God as a foundation for our lives, we live free from the overwhelming weight of it all because he is our ultimate strength, wisdom, and resource for everything. Isaiah 26:3-4 says, *"You will keep in perfect peace all who trust in you, all whose thoughts are fixed on you! Trust in the Lord always, for the Lord God is the eternal Rock."*

Our heavenly Father offers us peace in two ways. The first is through our salvation. In Jesus' sacrifice, we find hope and assurance that our sins are forgiven. By accepting Jesus as our Lord and Savior, we are accepting the gift of grace. We put our trust in God's faithfulness and his provision. Then, as Jesus followers, we stay in God's peace through our sanctification. Our spiritual growth is vital if we are to walk in the peace God offers us. Allowing the Holy Spirit to transform our hearts to become more like Christ, we gain unexplainable peace even in the trials of life. In Romans 15:13, Paul writes, *"I pray that God, the source of hope, will fill you completely with joy and peace because you trust in him. Then you will overflow with confident hope through the power of the Holy Spirit."* This is what I pray for every follower of Christ—that we never forget the hope and power we have in him.

CHALLENGE:

Are you looking for peace in all the wrong places? Take time today to surrender it all to Christ and receive the peace God has for you.

Ambassadors of Peace

"Therefore since we have been made right in God's sight by faith,
we have peace with God because of what Jesus has done for us.
Because of our faith, Christ has brought us into this peace of
undeserved privilege where we now stand, and we confidently
and joyfully look forward to sharing God's glory."
(Romans 5:1-2)

Throughout my teaching career, when my students would try to convince me to make things easier for them or give them answers, they would say, "But sharing is caring!" While they were always advocating for me to give them something that would provide an instant academic benefit, I always chose to respond with, "I do care! I'm sharing my knowledge!"

As benefactors of God's peace and wisdom, we should be excited to share what we know. Our stories of how we have experienced God's peace in the midst of hardship can become a beautiful and beneficial witness for others. Not only are we called to "*share each other's burdens*" (Galatians 6:1-2), but we are also expected to become ambassadors for the Kingdom. Second Corinthians 5:20

says, "*So we are Christ's ambassadors; God is making his appeal through us. We speak for Christ when we plead, 'Come back to God!'*"

To become an ambassador means we become a representative for Christ, appointed for a special purpose. And that is exactly what God has told us throughout the Bible. As Christ followers, we are all members of the body of Christ. He has given us all gifts and skills that can be used to serve others for his glory and to share the peace we have found through God's faithfulness. In Paul's letter to the Ephesians, he talks about the importance of spiritual growth and unity of the body. In Chapter 4, verses 15 and 16, Paul says we are to "*grow more and more like Christ*" and "*as each part does its own special work, it helps the other parts grow, so the whole body is healthy.*"

Our stories of God's love, faithfulness, and provision are important to share. We can use these personal stories to point others to God's glory and the gift of salvation through Christ. As we navigate our own trials, we become a witness for how we can still find peace and joy through the Spirit, knowing God is in control. If others see our hope and trust in our Savior, even when we are hurting, they will be more likely to trust us with their own struggles and doubts. We are then in a perfect position to point them toward our God of hope, kindness, and faithfulness.

CHALLENGE:

Is there someone with whom you need to share God's peace? Pray that God reveals to you anyone who could benefit from hearing your story.

11

Patience with Others

"Therefore I, a prisoner for serving the Lord, beg you to lead a life worthy of your calling, for you have been called by God. Always be humble and gentle. Be patient with each other, making allowance for each other's faults because of your love."
(Ephesians 4:1-2)

As is true for most teachers, my first year in the profession was a particularly rough one. Learning to handle all the details and chaos of the classroom felt overwhelming on most days. The students could be very difficult, always testing and pushing boundaries. They came to school with a variety of baggage, often placed in their lives by others in the home. Showing up every day and offering my best to them was not always easy. Giving them love and patience while they sometimes intentionally resisted it was challenging, both physically and mentally. I could see how this was an important moment for me to show the unconditional love of Christ. But in the moments of frustration, irritation and exhaustion, I admit it was hard to love them.

People can be difficult, and our sinful nature can compulsively react in unloving ways. Scripture tells us over and over again that we are supposed to love our neighbor, our enemies, and everyone else (1 Thessalonians 5:14). Paul gets even more specific in scripture, describing what love looks like. And do you know the first word he uses to describe it? "Patience" (1 Corinthians 13:4-5). To love others the way God intended, we have to learn to pause, pray and control our emotions.

The reality is that our sinful nature will always draw us into reacting with anything but patience. Others around us will constantly test our self-control, some even on purpose. Proverbs 14:29 warns, *"A patient man has great understanding, but a quick-tempered man displays folly."*

However, the calling still stands: as servants of Christ, we are expected to offer everyone patience and forgiveness (Colossians 3:12-13). Paul even reinforces the importance of exhibiting patience if we are to truly love others when he tells us to *"patiently bear with each other in love"* (Ephesians 4:2). So, how do we do it? How can we move past our impulses and learn to love the way Christ did, with unwavering patience? The key is in realizing, as with all the other fruit of the Spirit, that we cannot give others patience through *our* strength alone. We must allow the Holy Spirit to convict us to set aside our own feelings and love others as Christ loves them. By reading God's Word and his heart for all people, we learn to love everyone equally as his creation. We start to see each individual through God's eyes, viewing each person as someone who Christ died for and is no more or less worthy of God's grace and love than we are.

CHALLENGE:

Is there someone God has laid on your heart to have more patience with? Are you struggling to have patience with people? Pray for God to allow the Holy Spirit to give you a more tender heart through the gift of patience to those around you.

12

Waiting on God

"Let all that I am wait quietly before God, for my hope is in him. He alone is my rock and my salvation, my fortress where I will not be shaken. My victory and honor come from God alone." (Psalm 62:5-7)

Patience and waiting: two words that make us all cringe. Trying to be patient and wait for God's direction can produce the same feelings of anticipation and frustration. Even the early followers of Christ struggled in the waiting. In Galatians 5:5 Paul encouraged them saying, *"But we who live by the Spirit eagerly wait to receive by faith the righteousness God has promised us."* God will often call us to trust him and have patience as you wait for his guidance.

Maybe you're waiting for a job offer, direction on how to handle a broken relationship, or physical healing for you or someone you love. God's timing is perfect, and he calls us to wait with patience in knowing he is our hope (Romans 8:25). That means we wait with a good attitude!

Sigh That's the hard part.

I've walked through some frustrating periods of waiting. I tried to control the circumstances and fight against the path God had laid before me. But ultimately it brought me to my knees. I lost that fight. However, when I surrendered to his will and his calling, everything fell into place. The peace I felt in my life was amazing! If I had just had more patience in the waiting and trusted him with the plan for my life, these seasons would undoubtedly have been more bearable. If you are struggling to have patience in the waiting, pray for God to calm your anxiety and allow you to trust his plan. He will come to those who call upon his name!

CHALLENGE:
Are you trusting God in the waiting? Is all of your hope and trust in him? If not, pray that he would give you peace and trust in his faithfulness.

13

Patience in the Suffering

"We also pray that you will be strengthened with all his glorious power so you will have all the endurance and patience you need. May you be filled with joy"
(Colossians 1:11)

Early in my journey of motherhood, I suffered a miscarriage. It was a loss that I never expected, and it left me feeling raw. My emotions became heightened and sensitive to even the slightest words or actions of others. Since this experience, my eyes have been opened to so many more women who have suffered the same way I did, sometimes even later into pregnancy. In this world, we all experience suffering. Pain and sadness are part of this life. God never promised a life without it. But he does promise to be there with us (Isaiah 43:2).

I suffered mostly in silence, keeping my head in the sand until I couldn't breathe. It was a burden I didn't want to place on others. A large part of me just wanted to get back to "normal," to pretend it never happened. I prayed that God would just take the suffering away in an instant. The truth is that God does not expect or want us to suffer in silence. He calls us into an intimate relationship with him where we bring our hurt and pain. In times of trial, we can find rest in the arms of the Almighty. Hebrews 4:16 says, "*So let us come boldly to the throne of our gracious God. There we will receive his mercy, and we will find grace to help us when we need it most.*" After several months of resting in God's previous faithfulness for my life, he slowly restored my soul. As the days went on, his light of hope seemed brighter and brighter.

Accepting his grace means we are patient with ourselves. Oftentimes we find it much easier to offer patience to others. We tend to expect more from ourselves than we do the ones we pray for. God already knows the pain we suffer, but we need to bring our thoughts and fears to him in prayer. Even if you told him the same thing yesterday, tell him again today. By resting in God's faithfulness and grace in this way, we can begin to mend. Have patience as the Holy Spirit restores your soul. As he heals your wounds, there may be a scar, but if you trust him with your time, your prayers, and your life, he will give you peace and joy through even the hardest moments of life. Take the time to be still in the arms of your faithful Father (Psalm 46:10). When we are ready, he can turn our stories into a beautiful testimony to the power of Christ in our lives.

CHALLENGE:

Are you suffering in silence? Release all your pain to him and allow the Spirit to mend your wounds.

14

Kindness Through Grace

"As God's partners, we beg you not to accept this marvelous gift of God's kindness and then ignore it. For God says, "At just the right time, I heard you. On the day of salvation, I helped you." Indeed, the "right time" is now. Today is the day of salvation." (2 Corinthians 6:1-2)

Much of my time is spent trying to teach my kids to be kind to one another. Due to my own human nature, I, in turn, have also had to learn how to extend grace and kindness to them as they learn. It is a part of parenthood that I did not anticipate being so overwhelming. I expected it to come naturally. The reality is that a lot of things God calls us to won't come naturally—sometimes showing grace and kindness included.

Colossians 3:12 says, "*Since God chose you to be the Holy people he loves, you must clothe yourselves with tenderhearted mercy, kindness, humility, gentleness, and patience.*" Grace and kindness go hand and hand. To be gracious means you show kindness and courtesy to others. Acts of kindness are good but God calls us to a more transformative, often subtle or unseen kindness, one that comes from the grace we have received and desire to share with others.

God's gift of grace to us through Jesus' sacrifice was given even when we did not deserve it. In his kindness, he gives us unmerited favor through accepting Christ as our Savior (Ephesians 2:8-9). This grace and kindness, shared through the Holy Spirit, is what God gives. Then our salvation should flow into sanctification, a spiritual growth where we can share what we have received with others. As the Spirit helps us become more like Christ, we learn how to freely offer the grace and kindness we have received from the never-ending source of God. It is because of his strength and power that we genuinely desire to share true kindness with those around us, even when they do not deserve it.

CHALLENGE:

Is there someone specific God brings to mind who needs kindness and grace? Pray for God to provide you strength through his grace and kindness so you can share it with others.

15

Kindness Over Quarrel

"A servant of the Lord must not quarrel but must be kind to everyone, be able to teach, and be patient with difficult people." (2 Timothy 2:24)

I'm not the type of person who would intentionally pick a fight. Definitely not a physical one. But I can have pride over a situation or idea. My stubbornness and pride can lead me to speak unkind words to my spouse. Sometimes even words of hate that I would be too embarrassed to admit. My words can, and have hurt those around me. Being right can feel more important than being kind. However, all of those things that lead to hurt are a sign that we are allowing Satan to win the battle in our soul. It is a sign that we should be drawing closer to our heavenly Father who can remove things that cause hurt, to replace them with the fruit of the Spirit.

If you claim to be a servant of the Lord and a Christ-follower, then you have to be prepared to invite the Spirit to remove anything in you that does not bring God glory (Romans 8:7-9). Fighting in a spirit of pride, stubbornness or hate with another person becomes a stumbling block for our own faith walk as well as for those who look to us as an example of faith. Replacing those negative acts with kindness allows us to offer others affirmation and encouragement. It opens the door for us to make them feel seen and loved instead of torn down. Even when they spread words of hate, we must respond with words of love. God's love, kindness, and grace are the only things that have proven to win the war over what Satan spreads through this world. Proverbs 10:12 says, *"Hatred stirs up quarrels, but love makes up for all offenses."*

CHALLENGE:

Has pride or stubbornness taken control of your soul? Do you struggle to spread kindness more than hate? Give your soul fully to your heavenly Father to mold. Allow the Spirit to remove those things that do not bring God glory.

16

God's Kindness

"For he raised us from the dead along with Christ and seated us with him in the heavenly realms because we are united with Christ Jesus. So God can point to us in all future ages as examples of the incredible wealth of his grace and kindness towards us, as shown in all he has done for us who are united with Christ Jesus." (Ephesians 2:6-7)

Everyone loves to hear news stories where someone exhibited a selfless act of kindness to a stranger. Social media is filled with people who record themselves or others doing something nice for someone. Whether some realize and acknowledge it or not, kindness originated with God. It is his kindness that shows us how to be kind; it strengthens us to be kind to others (Proverbs 21:21).

His powerful and perfect kindness can be found throughout scripture. The heart of the Gospel comes out of his grace and mercy, and it is this demonstration of the ultimate level of kindness that we should strive to emulate and share. Jesus' life (and subsequent death) was the embodiment of God's kindness towards us. Titus 3:4

says *"When God our Savior revealed his kindness and love, he saved us not because of our righteous things we had done, but because of his mercy. He washed away our sins, giving us a new birth and new life through the Holy Spirit'."*

None of us are perfect. Nor will we ever be perfect. Accepting our salvation means we recognize that our Savior's sacrifice was needed in the first place and encourages us to turn away from our sin (Romans 2:4). Our heavenly Father's kindness towards us proves his faithfulness. It provides strength and hope for the future.

CHALLENGE:

Have you accepted God's ultimate act of kindness through Jesus' sacrifice? Pray that he opens your eyes to how you can spread his kindness to others.

17

Doing Good to All People

"Therefore, let us offer through Jesus a continual sacrifice of praise to God, proclaiming our allegiance to his name. And don't forget to do good and to share with those in need. These are the sacrifices that please God."
(Hebrews 13:15-16)

For as long as I can remember, any time I leave my parents, my dad has told me "Be good!" (which is his version of "I love you") before we part ways. Originally I was kind of annoyed by it. For a time I wished he could just go ahead and say the words "I love you" instead. But now I take it for what I know it is. Now, like many parents who repeat things said to them, I can't seem to help saying both phrases to my kids as we part ways. The phrases together, hopefully, become a reminder that they are loved, but also that they should always strive to do their best to be good. Our heavenly Father leaves us with this same message, saying that goodness should be a fruit of the Spirit in our lives. But what does God's biblical goodness look like? What does he really mean when he tells us to "do good"?

Ephesians 2:10 says, *"For we are God's masterpiece. He has created us anew in Christ Jesus, so we can do the good things he planned for us long ago."* We all have skills and talents our Creator expects us to use. If we come to him, asking what good we should be doing in his name, he will reveal the plan that he has always had for us—for our good and the good of those around us.

Whatever good God calls us to, he will require that we share it. The spreading of the gospel and its truth relies on followers of Christ sharing their entire lives and bodies for the Kingdom (Romans 12:1; 2 Timothy 2:15). Our stories of redemption are meant to turn into an outpouring of God's unending grace for others. In 1 Peter 2:9, Peter says, *"But you are not like that, for you are a chosen people. You are royal priests, a holy nation, God's very own possession. As a result, you can show others the goodness of God, for he called you out of the darkness into his wonderful light."* There is a battle going on between good and evil. Hearts and souls are battered by the darkness. Once we step into the light and hope of Christ, we are called to do good for others. Evil exists in this world, but we have the power of a God who has already won the battle over evil. He only asks that we hold tightly to good (Romans 12:9). Spread more light than evil to a world filled with souls that desperately need to see his face.

CHALLENGE:

What good is God calling you to? Pray for him to reveal to you how you can do good for God's glory.

18

God's Goodness

"Taste and see that the Lord is good. Oh, the joys of those who take refuge in him!"
(Psalm 34:8)

In the church I grew up in, our congregation would often use greetings in a call-and-response pattern. It became a habit for me that when any pastor would say, "God is good, all the time," I would respond, "All the time, God is good." As a young person, I did not fully understand the depth of those words. Now as an adult, when I hear or say those greetings, the richness of their truth speaks to me more than ever before. I know that God created good, does good for us, and calls us to produce good for his glory.

From the beginning, God has been good and created good (Genesis 1:31). This goodness included creating us in his own image. Since that day, he has proven himself to be faithful. Psalm 107:1 says, *Give thanks to the Lord, for he is good! His faithful love endures forever.* His steadfast, unconditional love becomes our strength in times of suffering. And even when this broken world brings us pain, he uses those times to ultimately create good for us in our lives (Romans 8:28).

Story after story in the Bible remind us of how good our God is. Through even our toughest phases of life, his Word is filled with endless examples of how trustworthy he has been and will always be for those who call upon his name. Nahum 1:7 says, *"The Lord is good, a strong refuge when trouble comes. He is close to those who trust in him."* Putting your trust and faith in him allows him to show you his goodness. He knocks on the door of your heart wanting to come in, but it is up to you to open the door (Revelation 3:20). He offers his goodness to us all, but it is up to you to open your heart to him. No matter what phase of life you are in or what circumstances you are experiencing, remember God's goodness. Give thanks for the good he has provided for your life and trust in his goodness for your future.

CHALLENGE:

Have you allowed God to bring his goodness into your life?
Thank God for his goodness and ask him to help you trust that
he will provide good for your future.

19

Others Over Self

"Don't be selfish; Don't try to impress others. Be humble, thinking of others as better than yourselves."
(Philippians 2:3)

I can be selfish, particularly when I feel like I have given more to others than to myself. My survival mode kicks in, and I become convinced that I should fight for what I want. Lashing out at my family is justified in my mind because, after all, they are the ones who are selfish, right? They are the ones zapping all my time and energy so I have little to nothing left for me. My sinful nature draws me into a bad attitude. Instead of others seeing God's goodness through me, they start to see the self-centered, unkind version of me.

The only way I have found to combat my selfishness is with the goodness and love God gives us, continually reminding myself that selfishness is not what God wants for me or those around me. He wants us to share his goodness with others. Time spent daily with my heavenly Father helps me see when my sin becomes a stumbling block for the devil to work in my life. God shines his light on my sin, convicting me, but also loving me through the process of forgiveness and change.

God knew we would struggle with selfishness. Jesus used many parables to teach his followers how to turn from their sinful ways and shine a light on God' goodness instead. Selfishness can bleed into so many areas of our life. But Jesus calls us away from that daily. He tells the crowd gathered in Luke 9:23, *"If any of you wants to be my follower, you must turn from your selfish ways, take up your cross daily, and follow me."* Christ knew this would be an ongoing battle for us.

It's not always easy to be selfless. We will stumble and struggle to move past our selfish mindset to show goodness and compassion to all. However, when we rely on what God has given us, focusing on the strength he provides, it becomes easier to shine for the Kingdom in even our most difficult relationships.

CHALLENGE:

Do you struggle with selfishness? Pray that God removes the selfishness in you so that you can better share his goodness.

Faithfulness

20

Faithful With Your Resources

"His master was full of praise, 'Well done, my good and faithful servant. You have been faithful in handling this small amount so now I will give you many more responsibilities. Let's celebrate together!'" (Matthew 25:21)

When I ended up having to resign from my teaching position in the middle of the school year, I was concerned about how that would affect my family financially. Pregnant with child number two and knowing the spending required with a newborn made me anxious. However, we had always done our best to be faithful with our tithe and to trust that God would provide if we followed his plan for our lives. My husband had already been job hunting, hoping to find a better paying position by summer. We wanted him to be established before I left teaching, but that did not happen. I had peace in the moment I resigned, but the realities of that decision filled my mind. Within a week of my resignation, my husband received a job offer. The pay was almost to the dollar what our combined salaries had been. God had blessed our faithful obedience with exactly what we needed.

Money is a sensitive topic that gives people a lot of anxiety and fosters a feeling of protectiveness. After all, it is our "hard-earned money," right? Human instinct is to want to spend what we have earned in the way we want to spend it. However, from a biblical perspective, that money is a blessing from God. As a matter of fact, all the resources we are blessed with are from a heavenly Father who loves us more than we can imagine. And he calls us to be faithful with what we have been provided. Malachi 3:10 says, " *'Bring all the tithes into the storehouse so there will be enough food in my Temple. If you do,' says the Lord of Heaven's Armies, 'I will open the windows of Heaven for you. I will pour out a blessing so great you won't have enough room to take it in! Try it! Put me to the test!'"* In response to God's faithfulness, we should be willing to give our resources back for his purposes. We should be excited to show our faithfulness to him by being faithful with our resources. In Matthew 25 Jesus says, *"To those who use well what they are given, even more will be given, and they will have an abundance. But from those who do nothing, even what little they have will be taken away."* (Matthew 25:29) When we use our provision well, God blesses our obedience abundantly. I know this because I have experienced it myself, over and over again.

Everything we have is a blessing from God—our house, our loved ones, our talents, and our money. However, when we talk of being good stewards, money is most often the first thing that comes to mind. While it is always good to tithe or donate to those who are acting as the hands and feet of Christ, we should remember that stewarding means more than offering a dollar amount. There is so much more to giving. And at the heart of it all is our posture of faithfulness towards our God. Hebrews 13:15 says, *"Therefore, let us offer through Jesus a continual sacrifice of praise to God, proclaiming our allegiance to his name. And don't forget to do good and to share with those in need. These are the sacrifices that please God."* Our heavenly Father provides all our blessings in the first place (Deuteronomy 8:18). In response, we must be trustworthy and willing to share with others, having an open heart of continued thankfulness (1 Corinthian 4:2). Bearing the fruit of faithful giving. After all, everything we have and everything we do should be used to bring glory to the Father.

CHALLENGE:

Are you being a good steward of all of God's blessings in your life? Have you thanked him for his abundant provision? Pray that he opens your heart and eyes to everything he has given you and then seek out opportunities where he is calling you to share those blessings with others for his glory.

21

Faith Over Fear

"This is my command--be strong and courageous! Do not be afraid or discouraged. For the Lord your God is with you wherever you go." (Joshua 1:9)

Through the years, when I would envision what my life would be like, I always saw myself as a working mom. As a child of a working mom, I saw what that looked like, and I never felt convicted to stay home with my kids. All that changed shortly before I became pregnant with my second child. During this time, I began to feel God nudging me to step back from my teaching position. These nudges grew stronger and stronger as the days went by, but I harbored an intense fear of becoming a stay-at-home mom. I didn't know how to do that! After all, it was God who had called me to teach, and I could not fathom why he would then call me away from that. I convinced myself that he would not ask that of me, and in my mind, all my fears surrounding that transition validated my reasoning. In the end, however, the nudges continued, and the conviction that I was allowing fear instead of faith to determine my decisions became clear.

In this ever-changing, high-stress world, it is easy for our souls to become burdened and our minds to lose focus. It is imperative during difficult times to remember that God is in control. He is not surprised by any of the chaos, and his plan will ultimately bless us. In practice, however, it is not always easy to push aside our fear and replace it with the certainty of God's faithfulness. If you read some of the many verses about fear, you will see that God urges us to "not be anxious" but to come to him in prayer (Philippians 4:6-7). He says that if we trust in him, he will give us peace (John 14:27).

Fear is one of the strongest tactics utilized by Satan. The only way to combat it is by trusting God's promises and provision. Our circumstances in life can become overwhelming and downright scary. Sometimes we can't even see a way out. We feel like we are drowning with no lifeboat in sight. The devil pulls us down with lies that tell us we are not enough and that our circumstances will never improve. 1 Corinthians 10:13 says, *"The temptations in your life are no different from what others experience. And God is faithful. He will not allow the temptation to be more than you can stand. When you are tempted, he will show you a way out so that you can endure."* When we lean into God's Word, he assures us that he is always enough. As we place our fears into his hands, relying on his wisdom and seeking his path, our lives will not only improve but will flourish in the light of his hope and strength.

To live in our faith more than our fear, we must cultivate a strong personal relationship with the God of hope (Romans 15:13). Daily prayer and reading God's Word keeps our hearts and minds centered on the assurance of who God is. With prayer and scripture as the solid foundation for our everyday lives, we are prepared to navigate whatever comes our way. The fear is defeated in the light of the gospel and in who we have fighting on our behalf. As we allow the Holy Spirit to fill us with the truth of God's faithfulness, we can push out the fear and ultimately prevent it from controlling our lives.

CHALLENGE:

Do you feel crushed by the weight of fear in your life? Pray that God reminds you of his faithfulness and allow him to replace your spirit of fear with the Holy Spirit, who can guide and encourage your heart.

22

Child-Like Faith

"I tell you the truth, anyone who doesn't receive the Kingdom of God like a child will never enter it."
(Luke 18:17)

Our two children want to be involved in everything! They love to follow my husband and me around, mimicking what we say and do. Like little sponges, they soak up anything they can learn from us. They often cannot even contain themselves from trying to be physically next to us as much as possible. Their trust in us is unshakeable.

The relationship we have with our heavenly Father should be the same. Like a child learning from a parent, Jesus becomes the model for our words and actions. We learn and grow spiritually with unbounded excitement, and in doing so, we faithfully draw closer and closer to our loving God, always seeking to trust him with our life and future. Matthew 18:3 states, *"Then he said, 'I tell you the truth, unless you turn from your sins and become like little children you will never get in to the Kingdom of Heaven.'"*

As children of God, we embody the analogy of sheep trusting the faithful shepherd (Psalm 23:1-6). Jesus, the shepherd of our souls, will protect us and provide everything we need if we allow him to do so. And even if we stray, he will never stop searching for us. This unconditional love that we enjoy from our shepherd is unmatched.

A critical part of our growth and maturity as Christians is learning to allow the Holy Spirit to mold us into being more Christ-like. Isaiah describes us as clay waiting to be fashioned into something useful and beautiful. If we are producing the fruit of faithfulness we will allow our Father to mold us into that purposeful vessel (Isaiah 64:8). This sanctification process is important in order to continually grow in God's righteousness for our lives. Our faithful willingness to seek him shapes the strength of our relationship with him. Jeremiah 29:13 says, *"If you look for me wholeheartedly, you will find me."*

Though we may struggle or stray, we should always be chasing after our heavenly Father, just as a child chases after its earthly Father. Take time to sit with him expectantly and soak up all his wisdom, trusting his love for you. Be like his child. And know that even when your own confidence wavers, you can always find rest in his fatherly arms.

CHALLENGE:

Do you feel like you have child-like faith? In what ways could you improve your relationship with your heavenly Father?

Gentleness

23

Gentle Teacher

"Take my yoke upon you. Let me teach you, because I am humble and gentle at heart, and you will find rest for your souls."
Matthew 11:29

When I was pursuing my teaching degree, a good deal of class discussion centered on teaching philosophy. We talked at length about the role teachers should play with their students. Above all else, my classmates and I were encouraged to act as guides for our students' learning. A successful teacher, we were told, gently leads each student through his or her individual learning experience. Our professors challenged us to create an environment of encouragement and compassion so that students would be open to receiving the instruction we had to offer them. Jesus epitomizes this type of teacher.

Jesus leads with kindness and compassion. The analogy of our Savior as the Great Shepherd is centered on this idea. As his sheep, he guides each of us, renewing our strength (John 10:14). His goodness and peace keep us safe even in dark valleys (Psalm 23). John 10:27-29 says, *"My*

sheep listen to my voice; I know them, and they follow me.
I give them eternal life, and they will never perish. No one
can snatch them away from me, for my Father has given
them to me, and he is more powerful than anyone else. No
one can snatch them from the Father's hand."

As the embodiment of God, Jesus experienced the same
things we do in this world. However, with God's wisdom,
he taught his disciples (and all those ready to listen) with
compassion. Matthew 9:36 says, *"When he saw the crowds,*
he had compassion on them because they were confused and
helpless, like sheep without a shepherd." John described him
as being *"full of grace and truth"* (John 1:14). His teaching
is still as relevant and powerful today as it was then. He
still extends grace, compassion, and wisdom to all of us. If
you humble yourself, allowing him to direct your path, he
will guide you through all of life's ups and downs. Christ is
the ultimate teacher, but we have to posture ourselves with
a willingness to hear and accept his words and promises.
Like sheep in a field, we must trust our shepherd to guide
us with his ultimate truth and wisdom.

CHALLENGE:

Are you open to the guiding hands of Jesus? Have you been
allowing Christ to provide wisdom and truth in your life? Pray that
you would be a willing student at the feet of your Lord and Savior.

24

Forgiving Others

"Since God chose you to be the holy people he loves, you must clothe yourselves with tenderhearted mercy, kindness, humility, gentleness and patience. Make allowances for each other's faults, and forgive who offends you. Remember, the Lord forgave you, so you must forgive others."
(Colossians 3:12-13)

I've had some relationships that have faded away or fallen apart. At one point I tried to bring a concern to someone whom I respected and felt close to. That relationship was never the same again. Perhaps I did not choose my words well. Perhaps, without realizing it, I had already hurt the person so much that the bond was too broken to be repaired. However, in the aftermath, I was wounded by their words. My feelings were hurt and my pride had taken a blow. I was angry that the conflict resolution I was hoping for did not occur. In the end, I wanted to forgive but struggled to do so. While I justified my actions and reactions by telling myself that my goal was to be completely honest (even through the use of a possibly less-than-loving tone), God revealed to me the importance of grace and forgiveness.

I'd love to say my heart quickly softened and forgiveness came easily, but it did not. Truthfully, I kind of fought it. My self-imposed righteous anger had taken root. However, after getting to a place where the burden of it was too heavy to carry any longer, I finally allowed God to carry it for me. I had to make the decision every day to give him my hurt and anger and then ask him to replace it with forgiveness. Once I allowed him to work in that space, he revealed to me that we are called to forgive in every circumstance, regardless of whether or not we ever receive an apology or a reconciliation. The unresolved conflict may remain unresolved because it takes willingness on both sides to fix a relationship. But even without a perfect resolution, we can and should forgive.

To be gentle, we have to learn how to overcome our sinful nature. Pride and selfishness will prevent us from showing gentleness through forgiveness. In 1 Timothy 6:11, Paul urges Timothy to pursue gentleness saying, *"But you, Timothy, are a man of God; so run from all these evil things. Pursue righteousness and a godly life, along with faith, love, perseverance, and gentleness."* If we are Christ followers who are striving to live the way our heavenly Father calls us to, then we are urged to do the same. We are to forgive others the same way we are forgiven (Matthew 6:14-15).

Our human nature, and that of those around us, will stir emotions within us that will be difficult to ignore. Sometimes it feels impossible not to get angry or bitter over what others say or do. We often react instinctively when we feel unappreciated or unseen. But Ephesians 4:31-32 says, *"Get rid of all bitterness, rage, anger, harsh words, and slander, as well as all types of evil behavior. Instead, be kind to each other, tenderhearted, forgiving one another, just as God through Christ has forgiven you."* The act of forgiveness can't be accomplished through our strength alone. Leaning into the God who forgave us first provides the example and encouragement needed to purge our anger and bitterness and to start the healing process of forgiveness. This takes time and daily prayer, but because God calls us to forgive, he will offer us the ways in which to do this. All we have to do is to be willing to open the door to let him in.

CHALLENGE:

Is there someone you have been struggling to forgive? Allow the Holy Spirit to relieve your soul of that burden and soften your heart to forgive as you have been forgiven.

25

Gentle Speech

"A gentle answer deflects anger, but harsh words make tempers flare."
(Proverbs 15:1)

I strive for open, honest communication in all my relationships. The way I see it, I could not keep my true thoughts to myself if I tried. My facial expressions and body language inevitably give me away. As much as I pride myself on being someone who will always be honest, God has revealed to me how I communicate that honesty matters. Words of encouragement and the tone of those words present a posture of communication and accountability where truth can be heard and dialogue can continue with love. God, in his kindness, has allowed me to learn these lessons through my husband, who highly values words of encouragement. While I innately share and see more value in *acts* of kindness, my husband holds tightly to my *words*. So, over time, I have come to realize the impact my words have, both good and bad. Through my husband, God has softened my heart to be cautious in how I express myself. Loving others well and in a Christ-like way depends on our openness to be gentle with our speech.

Proverbs 16:24 says, *"Kind words are like honey—sweet to the soul and healthy for the body."* Our words, and how we impart those words, matter because it affects the health of those to whom they are spoken. If our desire is to bring God glory in all we do, our speech is included in that—all of it! And if we are not careful, our speech will knock others down instead of building them up. We are called to build up and encourage each other with our words (Ephesians 4:29).

In James, chapter 3 includes an entire section on "Controlling the Tongue." James starts by talking about how our sinful nature can cause us to struggle. Verse 9 says, *"Sometimes it praises the Lord and Father, and sometimes it curses those who have been made in the image of God."* James goes on to say that the solution to our struggles in this regard is to seek God's wisdom and draw closer to him, allowing him to replace our sinful ways with the grace he offers. If we are not intentional with our words, ensuring that they are bringing God glory, then we are diminishing our witness to the world. Proverbs 15:4 says, *"Gentle words are a tree of life and a deceitful tongue crushes the spirit."*

God continues to impress on me how my words impact others. Some days or moments are easier than others. However, I must strive to continually relinquish my voice over to what he wants me to say. I pray that anything in me that does not bring God glory will be removed and replaced with the spirit of Christ. Seeking wisdom and intention with my words of choice in all circumstances has allowed me to avoid tempting moments where, in the past, words of pride and selfishness would have once been shared without hesitation. We are called to speak truth and love like Christ (Ephesians 4:15). And to do so, we must boldly ask our heavenly Father to help us turn away harsh words, replacing them with gentle ones.

CHALLENGE:

Are you allowing God to use your words for his glory? Do you struggle to use words that bring life to those around you? Pray for God to help you replace those moments of sinful instinct with Spirit-filled words instead.

Self-control

26

Anger

"A hot-tempered person starts fights; a cool-tempered person stops them."
(Proverbs 15:5)

In anticipation of becoming a parent, I expected to feel a lot of things: happiness, excitement, and even a sense of being overwhelmed. However, what I did *not* expect to feel was anger. Lack of sleep, lack of confidence, and lack of control over what I should or could do quickly brought out feelings I never would have anticipated. What others had told me would be the best days (days I would miss deeply in hindsight) actually perpetuated feelings of anger about how much I was sacrificing.

Even worse, I began taking out those feelings on my husband and daughter. My words were not always loving or sweet. I did not savor or enjoy the small moments of motherhood like I should have. Instead, my circumstances allowed Satan to get the better of me. The devil was turning this amazing blessing from God into a weakness he could exploit. In his kindness, God convicted me of my anger.

He called me closer into his arms. While I could not be the mother I wanted to be in my own strength, he reminded me that I could be the mom my child needed by pursuing a Christ-like life. He helped me find a way to turn those moments of anger and frustration into opportunities to share grace with those around me. As I spent more time daily in God's Word, pursuing his strength and guidance, my heart softened and my patience increased.

Anger can stir up quickly and make us lash out. Satan loves to harness it for his purposes, drawing us away from sharing God's love. However, the Bible makes it clear that we are to avoid anger, striving for righteousness. James 1:20-21 says, *"Human anger does not produce the righteousness God desires. So get rid of all the filth and evil in your lives, and humbly accept the word God has planted in your hearts, for it has the power to save your souls."* To successfully rid ourselves of anger, God calls us to fill our hearts with his truth and hope. The only way to overcome evil is with the goodness of God (Romans 12:21).

CHALLENGE:

Do you have things in your life drawing you into lashing out in anger? Pray that God will give you his strength and patience so that you can produce the righteousness God desires for you.

27

Listen More Than You Speak

"Understand this, my dear brothers and sisters: You must all be quick to listen, slow to speak, and slow to get angry."
(James 1:19)

I can talk...a lot. Awkward silence often prompts me to fill a conversation void, and I enjoy sharing helpful insights or suggestions with those around me. However, I have also spent many evenings cringing at the afterthought of how much I talked in certain social situations. As I have gotten older (and my husband has brought it to my attention), I now realize that by not allowing for pauses in a conversation, I may actually be doing the opposite of what I intend. Instead of enriching the dialogue and promoting two-way communication, it is quite possible that I am inadvertently making others feel unseen and unheard. My insecurity of clarifying what I meant by what I said, talking even more, just reinforces the fact that I am not allowing the other person to speak and be heard. Not only can our inability to listen well affect how well others feel loved, but it can also impact our ability to hear what God wants to reveal to us through others.

A humble heart, willing to listen and learn, pleases God. Making sure we hear what those around us are truly saying not only prevents them from feeling unloved but also allows God to use them as a vessel to share wisdom for our own benefit. Proverbs 18:13-15 says, "*Spouting off before listening to the facts is both shameful and foolish. The human spirit can endure a sick body, but who can bear a crushed spirit? Intelligent people are always ready to learn. Their ears are open for knowledge.*" God makes it clear throughout Scripture that there is wisdom in listening more than focusing on ourselves (Proverbs 12:15).

To fully pursue God's path for our lives and to obey his calling, we must keep our eyes and ears always focused on our heavenly Father. His truth and wisdom should be our ultimate source of help for everyday life. However, in order to hear what God is calling us to do, we must be willing and active listeners. Our faith relies on our ability to hear (Romans 10:17). We are all called to listen and trust the Lord. Isaiah 51:1 says. "*Listen to me, all who hope for deliverance— all who seek the Lord! Consider the rock from which you were cut, the quarry from which you were mined.*" Your creator calls you to listen and trust him with all that you are.

CHALLENGE:

Are you talking so much that you are not listening to others around you? Are you prepared to listen to God's instructions? Pray that God allows you to have a spirit (and an ear) open to receive his guidance.

28

Control Complaints

"Do everything without complaining and arguing so that no one can criticize you. Live clean, innocent lives as children of God, shining like bright lights in a world full of crooked and perverse people." (Philippians 2:14-15)

Complaining can be a hard habit to break. As a stay-at-home mom, I can easily be drawn into sharing how overwhelming and difficult my day has been. Often I wear my complaints like a badge of honor. I see myself as a true martyr, sacrificing all for the good of my family. I even tend to compete with my husband over who does more and who has the harder job. The "complain cycle" gains speed until we are both drained from arguing over which of us is more deserving of a break. This is not only bad for our marriage but it also keeps us from sharing the hope and encouragement of our faith. Instead of building each other up, we drag each other further down into a selfish, stubborn pit, complete with bad attitudes and hurt feelings.

God desires us all to have a heart filled with thanksgiving (1 Thessalonians 5:8). While Satan tempts us to be selfish,

God calls us to be selfless. He wants us to seek contentment and thankfulness for all he has provided. Complaining ultimately only drains our soul and negatively affects others around us. In God's Word, we are told to build each other up (Ephesians 4:29). Our words of love and hope are to shine for the world to see. Matthew 5:16 says, *"In the same way let your good deeds shine out for all to see, so that everyone will praise your heavenly Father."* As we praise our heavenly Father for his faithfulness, even in times of struggle, others can experience the hope and peace God has to offer us all.

To keep steadfast in your ability to share light over destructive complaints, remember God's blessings and faithfulness. Remind yourself how he has been faithful to you in the past, never forgetting how he has rewarded your obedience. Read God's Word, which is filled with stories of his faithfulness to his followers. Allow him to encourage your spirit so that you can be the light and hope for those around you.

CHALLENGE:

Have you ever experienced how your complaints draw others into the "Complain Cycle"? Pray that God helps you break that cycle. Remind yourself often of his blessings and faithfulness so that you can better share the hope we have through our heavenly Father.

ACKNOWLEDGEMENTS

First and foremost I want to give praise and gratitude towards God Almighty for allowing me to be a vessel for his words and truth. The inspiration and conviction by the Spirit which guided me along the way. To God be the glory as these words reach the hands of readers.

To my husband, Josh: Thank you for creating space in our lives for me to fulfill this calling God placed on my heart. Your encouragement and efforts to ensure its completion were invaluable.

To my parents: Your years of dedication to the Lord's work and instilling Christ into my heart has flourished into a faith which made this possible. It helped me have confidence in who God is and how he calls us to obedience for his purposes.

To Tina, Lisa, Sonya and Andrea: Your feedback, insight, and unwavering encouragement throughout this process helped pick me up when Satan tried to knock me down. It helped me finish well and gave me hope for how these God inspired words will be a blessing to others.

To you, the reader: Your support for my writing humbles me with an overwhelming gratitude. I pray God speaks his truth and love into your life. May his grace and hope fill your life through the words that fill these pages.

ABOUT THE AUTHOR

Casey is a wife and mother of two. She enjoys time with her family doing simple things like movie nights and cooking together. Her family lives in the suburbs of Atlanta, Georgia. Connect with her at **www.caseywayne.org**

SPOTIFY PLAYLIST

Use the QR code to access a special
Spotify playlist created by the Author!